SEASIDE BUNNIES
Life at the Beach

Minda Stephens

FOR

KEVIN
AND EVERY BUNNY WHO
LOVES THE BEACH
ENOUGH TO TAKE CARE
OF IT.

SEASIDEBUNNIES©MindaA.Stephens2024
ISBN: 979-8-9902555-7-9

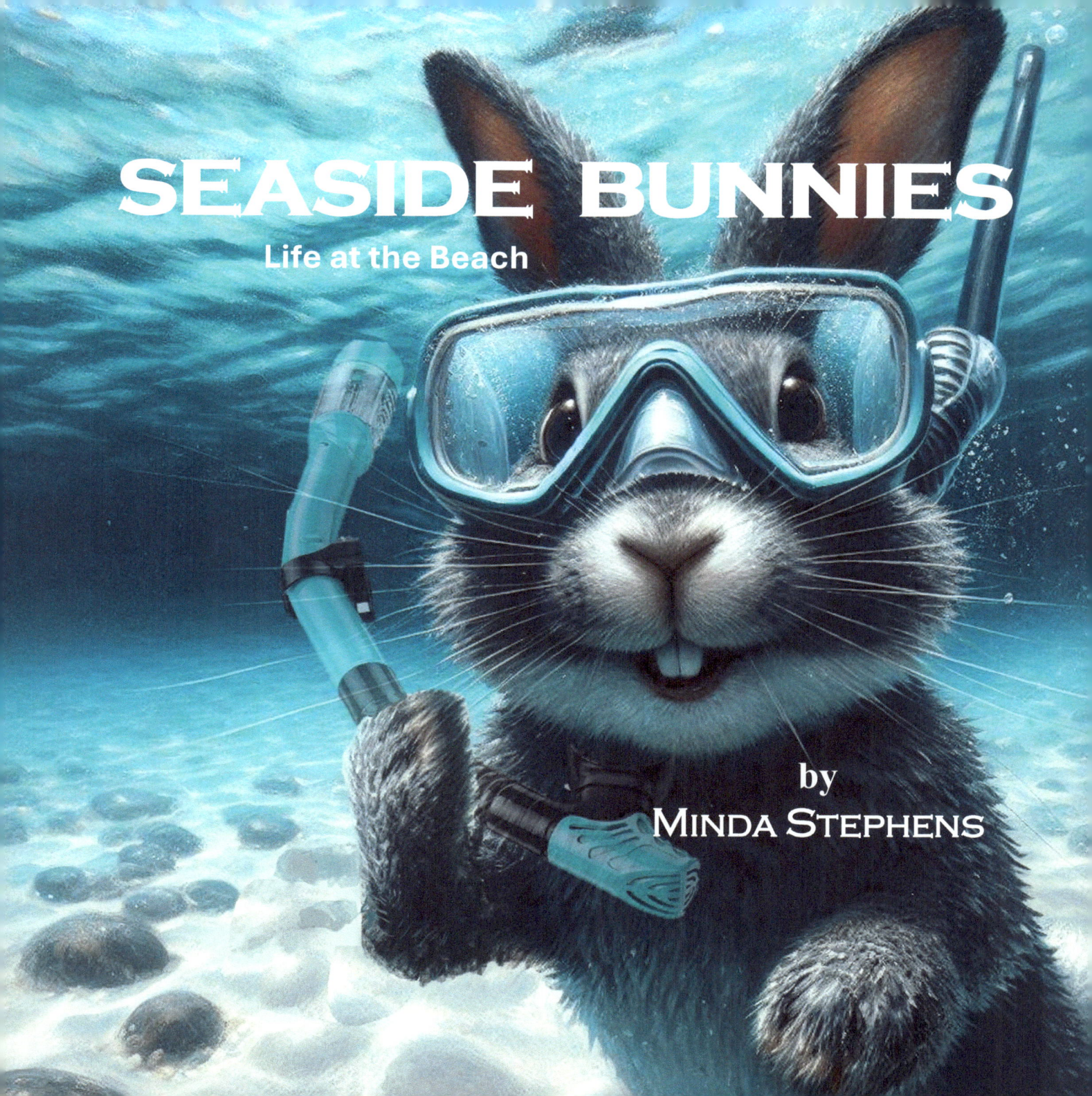

WELCOME TO THE BEACH !

**When you visit the coast for a seaside vacation,
You arrive as a guest of the Bunny Beach Nation,**

Because the seaside offers
so much to do,
There's a long list of things
and here's just a few:

Wake up to the sunrise and smile at the day,

Have breakfast at Grandmother's favorite café.

The seaside is a wonderful place to explore;

There's swimming,

and diving, …….

And walks by the shore.

You can build sandcastles,

Fly from parasails,

Go fishing with friends,

Or gather seashells!

Help Dad comb the sand with his metal detectors,

In search of lost jewelry,

and coins for collectors.

You can learn how to swim from a dock or a pier,

Or how to tread water with those you hold dear.

Ride a wave on a surfboard,

Go waterskiing,

Or slide on a skimboard, like a marsh hare that's fleeing!

STORMY WEATHER - STILL TOGETHER

When it rains at the beach it thunders and pours, but there's a lot you can do in a beach town indoors:

A movie,

An ice cream,

Or souvenir stores!

You can visit Great-Grandpa at his senior health center,

Shop for sunglasses,

Or go out to dinner.

**Stay with Aunt Elsie,
watch classic rom-coms,**

**Or go roller skating
with friends and their Moms.**

Do jigsaw puzzles

Tell jokes and make merry

Work out and build muscles,

Go to the library.

Now, talk to the bunnies who call the beach home.
If you do, then you'll find out you're never alone

Resort personnel
provide places to sleep,

While restaurant bunnies prepare meals to eat.

Spa bunny treatments

make you feel brand new,

While gallery rabbits sell Fine Art to you,

Jacque Lapin (b. 2016)
Reclining Bunny, 2018
Oil on canvas

If you need supplies,
there are water sports shops,

To buy everything from
dive fins to flip flops,

When the rainstorm has passed and it's sunny again, Get the all-clear from lifeguards,

Then jump in and swim!

Or soak up some sun and relax by the pool,

**Wearing comfortable clothes
to stay cottontail cool.**

Play ball in the surf !
Or,
better yet,

Teach someone to swim and they'll never forget!

SUN, FUN, AND SAFETY

Lying out on the beach
in the sea air is grand,

But make sure to have bunny sunscreen on hand.

These bunnies stayed out in the sun way too long,

And caused lots of worry for everyone.

Now it looks like there's finally a lesson well-learned,

They wear hats and sunscreen, so they won't get sunburned.

**Boat rides in the sea are a real dream come true,
But think _safety first_ and wear lifejackets too!**

When accidents happen to bunnies afloat,

Just call on the Coast Guard with their rescue boat!

HARES WHO CARE

Have fun at the beach, play without a care,
but always make sure that helpers are there.

If you get lost or hurt, don't be afraid,

Lifeguards and medics are here to give aide,

SAVE SEA TURTLES

These baby turtles just hatched in the sand,
   And bunny folk guard them from harm on dry land.
   They turn off night lighting from houses and porches,

   Then make sure their neighbors know not to light torches.
   So, the moon's light is shining as bright as can be,
   To guide hatchlings back to their home in the sea.

CLEANUP CREW

The beach is far more than parties and play,
It's a home that must be cared for each day.

This bunny uses a giant sand sifter,

To sort out beach trash with a big tractor lifter,

And volunteer bunnies from miles around,

Make sure that there's no litter left on the ground.

They all work together to keep the beach clean, save wildlife from harm, and sea plants pristine.

LET'S LEARN

There is so much to know about coastland and seas,
The subject is divided into specialties,

To learn about the life of the sea:
its waters, its tides, and its history,
study

OCEANOGRAPHY

the science of the life of the sea.

To learn about sea creatures and all their wonder, From the sky, shore, and sand, to the deepest blue yonder,

study

MARINE BIOLOGY

The science of life in *and* around the sea.

Remember:

Our oceans and beaches are living things,
   That give life year-round, from summers to springs,

There are seabirds that fly with grace in each feather,

   And pelicans catch fish in all kinds of weather.

There are jellyfish, and shellfish, and great coral reefs,
That float in the water and eat without teeth.

There are starfish, and garfish,
and crabs in abundance,

And elegant dolphins make each day a fun dance.

Now, when your
seaside sightseeing is through,
Come down to the shore,
there's one more treat for you.

SUNSET TOGETHER

Beach folk come together at the end of the day
To watch the best view of the sea on display,

As the sun's light moves on
to the rest of the world,
The sky turns bright colors and
sunset is unfurled.

Then everyone in the Bunny Beach Nation applauds in a seaside celebration.

And in native tradition,
some stand on the shore
To think of the day gone
and the night that's in store,

They look at the stars and give thanks for the sea,
And the life that it brings every seaside bunny.

**Enjoy all your days at the beach by the sea,
Protect and respect it so it will be,**

A home and a playground for you and for me,

And, of course, for every seaside bunny.

The End

www.ingramcontent.com/pod-product-compliance
Lightning Source LLC
Chambersburg PA
CBHW051514110526
44582CB00007B/123